LIVEABILITY

LIVEABILITY

Claire Orchard

Te Herenga Waka University Press
Victoria University of Wellington
PO Box 600 Wellington
teherengawakapress.co.nz

Copyright © Claire Orchard 2023
First published 2023

This book is copyright. Apart from any fair dealing
for the purpose of private study, research, criticism or review,
as permitted under the Copyright Act, no part may be reproduced
by any process without the permission of the publishers.
The moral rights of the author have been asserted.

A catalogue record is available at the National Library
of New Zealand.

ISBN 9781776920792

Printed by Blue Star, Wellington

Contents

Southern Regional Call Centre

There's snow falling and here we are, warm
in our glass, steel, ceiling tile and carpet square box,
talking on our phones and looking at it
drifting down and piling up on the street below,
on trees and lamp posts, cars shushing
thickly through it. So we imagine at least,
double glazing preventing certainty about
the exact sound. When did we get so tall?
When exactly did we first notice water birds,
so hearteningly unsinkable on lakes,
first notice lakes? Plucked from a scene in a film
those birds seem, dotted across a surface
we can see from here is presently iced over. Half
a gingernut drowned in my KeepCup makes no ripples
only sinks without fuss as deep as joy sometimes does.

If you take one piece of advice this year let it be

Impossible is nothing!
the T-shirt says and here you go,
I've not bothered to customise
the message. Actions speak louder,
our gran would say, swearing
by a good rinse off in the sea,
a gob of spit on insect bites,
her head-shaking advice
to never take the stairs two at a time
in either direction but especially not
on the downward leg,
to be sure to hold hands
at any crossroad, with the world
being in such a rush, and us being
unable to stop ourselves scratching.

Ambition

Of all the people I want to be I most want to be
Wilson Alwyn Bentley, cloud physicist,
the first person to photograph snowflakes.
When I'm a young farmer in Jericho, Vermont,
slight, yet as strong as anyone in the district,
I'll stand at my window, watching the storm,
waiting for its passing. Then, layered
in my warmest clothes, I'll go out
into the snow to hunt. Working fast,
I'll coax my prize onto a chilled blackboard
about one foot square, keeping my distance,
knowing a touch of breath could destroy,
knowing evaporation is a constant threat.
Back in my workroom, with the assistance
of a splint plucked from my mother's broom
and a turkey feather left over from Thanksgiving,
I'll manoeuvre the candidate into position
on its glass slide. Next, still be-mittened, using
a system of strings and pulleys I'll drag that icy dot
into focus, peering through my lens until satisfied
the likeness is as crisp as I can make it, whereupon
I'll expose it onto a sensitised glass plate,
in order to illuminate and hand etch the image.
Then I'll go out and do it all over again.
My father will think the whole thing
a lot of nonsense but I will not be told
and, loving me as he does, he will indulge me.
By the time I die, very old, having succumbed
to pneumonia, my collection will span
forty-six winters, will number in the thousands,
each a singular recording of the basic unit of snow.

Charms

Driving along Main Street the old places dangle,
unpolished, from a tacky tarmac chain:
the squat, grey-rock women's hospital,
the chipped and faded boards of our grandparents'
ex-state bungalow. The Baptist Church's cut-glass angles
now the River of Life Centre and, opposite,
my once-boyfriend's cubazoid, sunset brick-and-tile
studded with net-curtained windows.

The centrepiece of the collection, the high school, has
sustained some major alterations. The maths prefabs
have gone. The science labs, solid concrete blocks
that surely should have stood monument forever,
have been razed, entirely replaced by a rectangle-cut gem
of emerald grass set with three saplings.

Doubling back, I drive through the front gates
that, according to the sign, should be locked by now.
But tonight the car park is full;
something's going on in the hall. Parent–teacher
conferences? Careers night? At a crawl I complete
the full circuit, passing the marae, the special needs unit;
both seem to have shrunk. At the exit, the mural
on the road-facing wall is unchanged,
its violently erupting volcano still showering
that unnamed wahine in ash and steam, her face
still wearing that vague, unfinished look.

Pulling up to the roundabout there's a faint figure
looming in the dusk, a teenage girl running
in front of my car. Her mate hesitates, looking
directly at me. I smile and wave at her and, although
she still seems unsure, she goes anyway.
I pass them, still running, pleated tartan skirts
flying. And then there's those god-awful imitation windmills,
a final faded pair of geegaws, smaller from this angle.

Furnace

for Agata

My room at one end of the block, on the second floor,
five staircases in all, ten flats to each staircase,
and we lived in the first. I'd never use the official route
to school – the pavement beside the road, heavy
with exhaust fumes. I'd take the shortcut – across the grass,
an informal track worn by the soles of our small,
fake-fur-booted feet. We'd duck through the hole in
the wire fence. You can't do that anymore, now it's concrete.
The sports field was surfaced with red brick gravel.
The boys would play football, the girls would practise
their long-distance running, running in wide circles.
We called our religion teacher Goat. He was very boring.
We had to learn things by heart. The class monitors were
in charge of wiping clean the blackboards, restocking
the chalk, locking up the coats and boots in metal cages.
I had a short hippy phase, 1993ish: long hair, bell-bottoms,
beads and round-framed glasses. Yes, I may have been
a cool kid then. I remember the old school had linoleum floors
but the new part had marble. It was slippery, that marble.
Once, against my dad's advice, I wore slippers, the ones
my aunt made me, to school. I loved those slippers.
Because of them, I fell on the stairs, chipping my front tooth.
See, right here. It was the only time I remember my dad
beating me, although he denies it and also my mother
believes it's impossible, says he never would do that.
I have no idea. Maybe they're right. All this happened
on this small piece of land. My parents still live there.

Unravelling things

That Ernest Rutherford is a past member of the Manchester Literary
and Philosophical Society I learn from studying the plaque
in the hallway of their new headquarters. I'm just in time
for a public lecture on John Dalton's atomic theory of 1803
as it relates to our current understanding of atomic physics.
Today's speaker is a man I've never heard of, but as he has

the voice of my grandfather I'm inclined to listen when he says
all matter – you, me, in fact everything in this room – I'm looking
now at the dyed-brown hair on the back of the head of the woman
in front of me – is composed of atoms. Well, almost everything,
he tacks on apologetically. The sound of my voice, your thoughts
and feelings about what you're experiencing – he shakes his own

balding head – these are not things, at least not in the atomic sense.
He moves swiftly on – there will be time for questions at the end –
to the big bang, that mysterious event, thirteen-point-seven billion
years ago, when pure energy was converted into elementary particles.
He pauses, shuffles his notes; here come the meat and potatoes.
The first part of John Dalton's atomic theory states that atoms

are indivisible and indestructible. Of course – he says
with a downward twist of his lips – we have accepted
for a while now this is not the case, that a nuclear reaction
can create or destroy matter, given of course we define matter as solely
its mass and not the energy such a reaction releases. As far as we know,
energy cannot be created or destroyed; it can only be transformed

from one state – hand gesture, a sweep left to right – to another.
We also know that, when we die, we become the quintessential
recyclable: our atoms, released – opening hand movement –

merely relocate to new real estate, allowing us to become perhaps
part leaf, part stereo dial, part some soft, small animal, this time
one with a tail. In this sense, we are only ever on loan to ourselves,

all of us having, at some time, been part star and who knows,
someday – wry smile – we may be again. He stops to check
his watch. Time now for questions and I sense there are many.
That, as usual, there will not be time enough to answer them all.
The man next to me wonders aloud if time passing is another non-thing,
in an atomic sense. If only getting to know these things felt like enough.

There are worse things

Christmas day in a four-berth caravan
in a corner of the Waipoua Forest public car park,
six humans and an over-excited, farting bull terrier.
Opening parcels, I don't care what anyone else got

because I've got *Grease* – the soundtrack double album! –
and I'm riding with it in the back of the Vauxhall Cresta,
opening and shutting the inside spread of film stills
until, inevitably, my brother punches me in the arm.

Rizzo is my favourite. Man, she's no Patty Simcox,
wannabe Carnival Queen. I like the way
she stands up to Kenickie. And Danny.
Hell, she stands up to everyone.

Three more long days of hugging the left, of tight
corners on hill roads, caravan bounding along behind,
to arrive at Uncle Jim's in Waipukurau, his vast
country music collection and his record player.

I'm putting on side one before the jug's even boiled
and I'll play it over and over, alternating
with side two until, inevitably, everyone else
clears out of the lounge room. Eventually, I figure

I may as well try one of Uncle's Gene Pitney albums.
Gene seems convinced the man who shot
Liberty Valance was bravest of them all,
but my money's still on Betty Rizzo.

Shooting rats

Uncle Jim drove the ute
and the dogs sat up eager in the tray

with the guns. Ten k's out of town
we turned off tarmac onto a farmer's

wet grass and up, up, we lolloped,
scattering sheep, eating

the juicy curves of the hillside
with all four wheels wide open until

reaching the top felt like flying
and when we looked we saw

through limbs of thinned macrocarpa
the sky, too, was planning something big.

Summers were longer then

This firebreak we're scaling
is dry and grit-slippery, just like
the one behind the side door
of the primer three classroom,
the one Mr Davis
of the wispy moustache
would have us clamber up
every fine morning
of the late summer term.

Some could manage two legs
but I was always on all fours,
feeling my way and the fear
of losing my grip, always
imagining myself
slow-motion tumbling,
collecting classmates
along the way

or just free-falling
between them, and them
stopping, open-mouthed,
to watch me plummeting,
the warm, rough concrete
of the netball court
rising up to kiss me hard.

Thursday night

Seven-thirty *Star Trek*, the fifth episode
of the third season, an encounter with Kollos,
Medusan representative of a telepathic species
so ugly the mere sight of one drives any human
instantly insane. By the second ad break
the *Enterprise* is, of course, wildly off course,
utterly lost. By the third a mind meld between
Kollos and Spock has been successfully executed,
the ship guided back to the relative safety
of known space. With everything more or less
happily resolved there's the usual moment,
right at the end, for musing upon
what we have learnt. The scriptwriters gift
this task to Kollos. Speaking from Spock's mouth,
he begins by praising the admirable
compactness of the human body, the impressive
range of our senses, the remarkableness
of language, happy reminders of the fine
specimens we are. When the camera zooms in
for a close-up on Leonard Nimoy's face,
it's as if he's speaking directly to us,
as if when he turns his attention to the way
these same features confine and confound us,
he's seeing through the glass screen into
our sitting room as he laments the bleakness
of such an existence. As if he observes
the widening of our eyes, poor lonely creatures,
perpetually at opposite ends of the couch,
and our mother, in her chair next to the fire.

Wild life

One time, Phillipa brought her pet geckos,
Romeo and Juliet, to stay the weekend.
The pair of them were living together
in an ice-cream container with holes
punched in the lid, furnished with
torn-up clumps of grass, a few leaves,
a couple of small twigs. Phillipa was quite a lot
older than me, was maybe fourteen, and knew
all sorts of stuff, like how to keep wild geckos
alive in an ice-cream container, how to make
a wholegrain loaf of bread from scratch
and how to get into heaven. I know this
because she showed me how to bake that loaf and,
when Romeo died suddenly that Sunday afternoon,
quietly rolling onto his narrow back
inside his bright blue plastic box and lifting
his four tiny green feet skywards, Phillipa
said his soul wouldn't go to heaven because
he was only an animal. Only people's souls
get to go to heaven she said, and even then
only the souls of people who had accepted
Jesus Christ into their lives as their Lord
and Saviour. She also told me if you add
'I ask this in the name of our Lord, Jesus Christ'
to the end of your prayer then, according to John
14:14, Jesus is contractually obliged to grant your wish.
Perhaps that's not exactly how she said it
but that was my takeaway. I asked if I could watch
when she asked for Romeo's resurrection but Phillipa
shook her head and said oh no, she'd not be
bothering God with stuff like that. That Romeo
had had a good life and would be staying dead.

Hold tight

For all our hard work, our claim
turned up dry. Day walkers had taken
over the hills, setting chattering fire
to the paths. It was all too much
like being at home. We retreated
into the bush, turning each other
around and around until we could not tell
which way. We thought ourselves daring,
dog-paddling from mainland to island,
scooping up tiny fish to hold, loosely caged,
in our mouths. Our hands blossomed pale
instruments full of air: hollow-boned flutes,
driftwood saxophones, an oddly beautiful
guitar from the picked-bare spine of a fish.
Handfuls of fine, sloppy clay scooped
from the creek bed we pounded flat
and shaped into the forms of sleepers,
quiet babies we would rock, hold tight
and smeary against our bony chests.

Deep Fake

In the window
of the fancy china shop
on the high street,

right in the middle
of the display shelves,
three white porcelain rabbits

imprisoned behind glass,
each no bigger
than a man's thumb,

each with shiny
brown eyes and
a small, pale-pink nose.

One stands tall
on its hind legs,
as if sniffing for foxes.

Another crouches down,
as if nibbling
lush grass.

The third lies
stretched out on its side,
legs long, as if relaxing in the summer sun.

Bird flight, in nature
films limited by
edges of flat screens,

in the wild continues
until the birds themselves
can no longer be seen,

although we know they are
somewhere out there, unobserved,
still flapping their wings.

Meanwhile, in Italy,
a triangle of hillside
recently planted with olive trees

slopes from right of view
to where it is interrupted
by the upright oblong

of a pyramid-roofed bell tower
with an archway below
where the bell balances ready,

the church attached
by a single-hipped shingle roof
and, next to the church,

a man in rolled shirt sleeves
and dark suit trousers,
about to go in and make his confession.

You might have heard the story of the snake
who swallowed a small dog whole,
in a single gulp.

The family returned to find the snake
tethered to the bike rack outside the market
by a length of red leather leash,

its mostly slim body laid out full length
and, protruding halfway along,
a tell-tale small-dog-sized bulge.

Hansel and Gretel: the media briefing

We all agree on this much:
everyone would like
a happy ending.

However, realistically,
we cannot expect the children will be in
precisely the same state of health as when we last saw them.

We have had a nasty rash
of wicked witches hereabouts and
if they have fallen prey . . .

well I'll put it this way:
we cannot expect they will be
unaffected by such an ordeal.

Personally, I'd like nothing better than
to find the little tykes
safely nestled

next to a tree stump
in the woods,
of course I would,

but we're law enforcement
not Santa Claus. On a good day
we catch the occasional burglar.

This is no reason
to give up, or at least
it is not a reason to despair.

Studies have shown
children to be
remarkably resilient:

like India rubber,
                                        they bounce
right back.

Xanadu summer album

Brother, do I remember you dismantling
that rotting tree house, dropping
that plank with the rusty nail
on my head. I remember
there was a lot of blood
left behind on the beach towel
Mum pressed to the wound
but it only took the doctor
three tiny stitches to close me up again.

You claim not to recall any of this.
We do agree on the long days of digging
down into wet sand, patting walls into shape,
fetching seawater in plastic buckets.
I say I think that was mostly me,
going to and fro, to and fro
but you just shrug and smile and turn the page.

Look at our skivvies, pegged by their hems,
skinny arms waving frantically in the wind
beside heavy, candy-striped sheets, pilled and scratchy,
flapping on the mānuka-propped clothesline.
The way the dog would slink inside
to lie on her side, her soft tummy turned to the fire.

Remember the derelict, one-room schoolhouse,
its empty playground cracking with weeds,
its small playing field unmown. We peered
through the windows at dark-stained wooden chairs
and desks in disarray, textbooks scattered across the floor,
the last lesson still chalked up on the blackboard.

Hmmm, you say. What about the way
the last of the daylight would turn
the iron roof of the long drop into silver?
And I wonder how you even remember things like that.

The Thing Is

Put it in the Trunk, he'd say,
meaning the Boot, of course
and I'd manage to lie

Everything down in there,
neatly folded. Then I'd close
the Boot. Masts hold Sails

upright, are handy for
stringing Flags up too, for
signalling. We used to fly

a Pennant from our Car Aerial
but it was not the Same. It said
Coromandel. Or Something.

Anyway. I have culled many
of these. It's Nothing Serious,
Doctor, I said to her and she,

believing me, gave me Nothing
for it but Time and Attention,
which was Sufficient. Armchairs

are only called Armchairs because
of their Arms. Chairs without
Arms are just Chairs. We never

think of it. This is often
where the Trouble starts, from
not recalling Details such as This.

Where duty lies

It seems my great-grandmother
and my grandmother did not get on,
even though (or perhaps in part
because) one fell in love with
and married the other's son.
Yet, when the time came,
the younger passed on to me
the elder's Sunday School award
she'd kept safe through six weeks
sea voyaging and forty-odd years
up and down the country on trains.
A novel by Silas K. Hocking,
gilt embossed, illustrated, awarded
in 1899 as first prize to nine-year-old
Annie Entwhistle of Albert Road
Congregational Sunday School
for punctual attendance
and good behaviour. And indeed
what more could be asked or expected?

Going home for Christmas

Outside the porthole the night is warm
and full of stars. In the overhead locker
your carry-on is stuffed with wishes.
Slip off your shoes,
punch up an inflight movie, relax.

No doubt Aunt Bea will make her
usual point of reminding you rain only falls
to empty the clouds, that any benefit
to the grass is purely incidental.

No doubt she'll bring, as usual, her ageing
Chihuahua, Raoul, who each year
selects someone to bite. The family
goes wide, looming from great heights.

You're wishing now you'd made more
progress since your last visit, had learnt
to ride a horse, or a bike, or at least managed
to memorise the lyrics to that song from *Frozen*.
There's no way there's still time.

II

December

Time again
to contemplate
moving to Vancouver.

Sure, the average temperature
looks chilly in winter,
and not very warm in summer,

and there are a lot of rainy days
between November and March,
but there are all those great beaches

and isolated hiking trails
and who wouldn't want to live
in a city that has been ranked

in the top five for liveability
and quality of life
for ten consecutive years?

And then, of course,
remember,
there's the ice hockey.

Staining baby

We take a moment to size up a chunk of it
before you start at one end, me at the other.
I wield the wide brush
and grip tight the wire handle
of the dangerously swaying bucket.
You have the narrow brush
and hold fast the small pot
with the fixed and sturdy handle.
When my wrists weary
of moving stain back and forth,
of forcing it into all the folds of skin
all the curves and whorls,
when I start worrying I might
drop the bucket, we swap equipment.
Stopping for a moment to contemplate
the section we've finished, I see
the effect is just as we'd planned
and I'm feeling hopeful we'll finish the job
although undoubtedly it's proven
a bigger affair than either of us anticipated
and realistically, looking at how far we've come
and how far we still have to go, we're going to need
more stain, more stamina, more days together.

Heartland

From the outside the Railway Hotel
looks promisingly Victorian chic.

Inside they smile lovingly at each other
over their children's tousled heads,

admiring the original kauri staircase,
intricately carved.

On the first-floor landing
the smell is engulfing;

someone is cooking something
nostril-piercingly pungent. But

their suite's on the second floor anyway,
they encourage each other,

and carry right on up, turning
their key in the lock at the end of the hall.

This looks like one of those places
on American TV, the ones where

people get shot then slide down the wall,
the twelve-year-old announces.

The double-hung window
has an expansive view

of railway tracks and, beyond that,
the main drag out of town.

Our son of eighteen summers

put our Toyota of ten
under the back of a bus
at the Basin Reserve
the afternoon of the day
we flew to Dunedin.

That night he called
while we were eating steak
and drinking wine
and his voice explained:

the bus stopped dead
while I was checking
my blind spot.
Then the cops (who happened
to be passing) stopped too,

wrote me a ticket,
while all the passengers
got off and walked away
in different directions.

Pizza night

for Jack

You don't need to look at the sides.
You don't need to look at the dessert menu.
You haven't even looked at the pizzas yet.

We can't leave the pizza page
until we've ordered pizza. You're like
what shall we eat tonight? Let's get pizza!

And then, all of a sudden, you wanna look at the sides.
Madness! How about I tell you what you need to know
and you make an informed decision.

Topography

We're here now and it seems we will not be turning back
(although yes, it would have been easier to walk along the road)

but will keep to this overgrown, slip-prone track,
only sometimes looking down at the way the holes

we've forced into the mud with our booted feet
are settling into murky parables. Our chattering voices

bring the birds down to voice their protest
at our invasion, our ineptitude. The Byzantine Empire

went through periods like this. Hard times of decline
followed by eventual recovery. And oh, the relief! All things

considered eventually go away again, that is the way
of all things you remind yourself, stepping deeply

into another crusted reservoir of mud, crud forming
a thick curd on your left sole. And then there's the rushing

noise of the road again, a flavour of wood smoke in the air
from the chimney of a nearby house. You hope

no one notices the faint whistle whooshing from
between your teeth as the black mouth of the cave recedes.

Discuss

Patience, as a virtue, is problematic. A case
in point: that smaller baby sat up weeks earlier
than its much larger, more laid-back compatriot.

There will be no dead body swamp in this poem.
No one will get trapped in an ancient orchard
with only red plums to survive on. Red is not
the only colour plums can ripen into. I mean,

you could groom that dumb horse daily, but
it would still not enjoy carrying you around
on its back. Some horses are smart like that.

The worst-kept secret

I found it lying, shabby
and flat on its back in the front yard,
on that patch of grass there
beside the fence. I'm glad you ask
because that I can't tell.
I've never been much
of a teller. When the weather
got warmer, a troop of Mounties,
all scarlet coats, wide-brimmed
felt hats and brown leather belts,
came thundering down
from their Canadian hilltops,
snatched it right from my hand
and galloped away with it laid,
like a folded blanket,
across their sergeant's saddle.
The parking warden,
who saw the whole thing,
looked at me
and I looked back
and neither of us said a word.
Ask him for his version, if you like.
He'll tell you. The worst secret
is the one you can keep.

Helicoptering

I'm at my desk, daydreaming
a scenario in which, instead
of requiring regular inhalations
of oxygen to stay alive, we have to
breathe in the ease of others to survive,

when I hear the wup wup wup
of the helicopter hovering overhead,
a sound that always makes me think
of people who have fallen badly
in the wilderness of Te Urewera,
of Vietnam and that never-met uncle,

but a quick check out the back window
reassures me it's just Judi next door
moving her electric Flymo methodically
across her small rectangle of lawn;
she looks happy enough.

Freeze frame

Turns out they are not at all alike, turns out
there is active dislike between his forehead,
pressed hard into the metal door jamb,
and her hair, clouding about her upside-down face.

Like trees in the wind, their expressions lately
have depended on the weather.
Experts at two-toned moments
and raised eyebrows on the bypass, disharmonious
silence rumbles in the valleys of their bed,
wild wheels scribing circular tracks
in their heads. Down dark gravel roads
they have careered to end up here,
dangling, engine and all,
halfway over this precipice. It's not healthy

for living things to live close to such unforgiving edges.
When the wind drops, their yellow places
start up, calling through the stillness
for reverse gear or, for pity's sake, a rope.

Results sorted by relevance

The art of gift wrapping, the art of strategic interviewing,
the art of lying, the art of digital branding. The art of strip
photography, of beef cutting, of the gut.
The art of integrative counselling, of fashion draping,
of not making. The art of British rock.
The art of capital restructuring, of readable code,
of pop-up. The art of getting by, of package design,
the art of the woodcut. The art of the salon, the art
of slow reading, the art of immersion, of coercion.
The art of the garden, of the accusation. The art
of recklessness, the art of the kiss. The art of insanity,
of *Toy Story 3*. The art of theatre, of worship.
The art of funding and implementing ideas. The art
of war, the art of cruelty, of software innovation.
The art of embroidery, of deceleration. The art of golf.
The art of choosing the art of tomorrow. The art
of folding, the art of rebellion, the art of a map,
the art of clinical supervision. The art of the LP,
of ecology, the racing motorcycle, the body.
The art of convening, the art of tapa, of literary thieving.
The art of taonga, of punk. The art of *Footrot Flats*,
of Peter Siddell. The art of helping others, the art
of storytelling, the art of motivating students
for mathematics instruction. The art of thinking, the art
of art therapy, of information security. The art of the first fleet.

Unrequited

My wide open eyes are fixed upon your face,
red and sweating, as your clasped hands
pound away on my chest.

Resuscitation involves
so much stress for both of us,
don't you think? You, demonstrating

yet again to the punters on their six-hour
refresher course, me here on the floor,
the back of my plastic scalp

pressing ever so slightly deeper
into the olive green and scratchy carpet
with your every compression – rescued from

death again! Hurrah! I revive and float away,
above you, above your students
watching you so intently.

I want to tell you
I despise you, knowing
you'll never feel the same.

A measure of rain

In the tradition of mermaids selling
bags of wind to becalmed sailors,
the city installs a precipitation room.

Citizens are invited to visit
and make exhibitions of themselves
so she goes to find herself surrounded

by rain falling through hundreds of tiny holes
drilled in the ceiling. Stretching out her hands
she discovers the point at which she ends

is precisely where the rain begins,
that she has become immune, transformed
into a fuzzy cloud, casting soft, silvery shadows.

And so she asks a stranger to take
a snap of her against the backdrop of deluge
to immortalise it resolutely falling where she is not.

While she waits for them to line up the shot
she rests herself within herself, appreciating
the monumental beauty of this

manufactured rain pouring down, of her being
in the middle of it not getting wet,
of feeling like an artefact

of mythic and ancient origin,
which is precisely
what she has always been.

Room

The chair, beige linen, wingback,
a little light wear to the places the head
and the arms rest, is next to the bed,
which is unmade (a rumpled blanket,
cream wool with a charcoal double stripe).
The lamp, switched on, small, round, bright
orange shade, on the desk in the corner
where there is another chair, oak,
straight-backed, ladder-backed,
pushed in. Hanging from its finial knob
a fine linen shirt, white, sleeveless,
hooked and dangling.
The morning light through
the open French windows is touching
all of this but especially highlighting
the filmy white curtains, the polished floorboards.
The climber scaling the railings of the balcony
is mostly thin, leggy stalks now, has lost
most of its leaves. The door, barely visible
to one side, is just the suggestion
of a door really, and a door handle.

After one storm, before the next

Packing sandbags, hand over hand,
against the crumbling bank. Some days
it all dribbles away, although
they say the human brain
retains everything somewhere or other,
if I only knew exactly where
my subconscious laid it down
and the noise rain makes on a corrugated-iron roof
when heard from beneath the covers of a warm bed
is still the best sound in the world.
Opening drawers, things overflow,
and where to start? Chickens come home
to roost but what of these mental bantams,
flapping about? Sometimes, moving in the shiny
eye of it, I'll catch sight of your photograph
and I'd swear you're just some model
I've never met, posing with a full wine glass
in an interior design magazine.

When I bring up advance care planning

Mum says oh yes, I keep changing my mind
about whether or not I want to be cremated
and I say Mum, once you're gone you won't care
and we'll just do whatever we want.
I'm not talking about after you're dead,
I'm talking about when you're still alive,
about what you want us to do if you can't
speak for yourself, if you're unconscious
or can't understand what's going on anymore.
Oh she says. Well, I don't want to be put in a home,
that's for sure. Unless there's no other option.
So, if the only other option is being dead,
you'd rather a home? Yes, I think so.
I really don't want to be in a home
but I suppose if it's that or being dead
then I'll have to consider it.
Mum, I'm talking here about when
you won't be able to consider it.
Like, do you want to be kept alive
if there's a good chance you won't wake up,
and if you do, you'll not be able to wipe your own bum
or feed yourself? What if you can't recognise people,
if you can no longer hold a conversation?
What if you have a massive stroke, and then
you stop breathing, would you want CPR?
Do you want artificial ventilation if you can't
breathe on your own? These are the sorts of things,
the kinds of scenarios you need to consider
and then tell us what you want us to do.
I suppose so, she says doubtfully.

Just looking

I didn't meet a soul until I met Rose
outside the auction house. We agreed
on the way in to be on our guard for
unfamiliar protocols. Most of the lots
were laid out on vast wooden tables.
Some were still in cardboard boxes
on the floor. There were stacks of dusty
beige or red leather-bound books,
vinyl-encased encyclopaedia sets, plates
in piles, bone china floral tea sets, silver
candlesticks, a pokerwork folding table,
mahogany sideboards, an ugly pair of white
ceramic Wally dogs, a lucky rabbit's foot.
We did not see any silver stags, although
I was momentarily, inexplicably tempted
by a pair of faded prints depicting
kilted Scottish clansmen, one Campbell,
one MacGregor. The regulars began unscrewing
thermoses, opening and arranging their snacks.
We stood together at the back, keeping our hands
at our sides, and the afternoon rattled along
to the rolling rhythm of the auctioneer's voice,
the regular rap of his gavel. Our valuation
assumptions were unfailingly way out.
Items we thought would be worth the most
went for less, and vice versa. Walking home
we looked up to see white-gloved contrails
rearranging the furniture in the atmosphere.

Contact print

I've spent a lot of time this week
looking through the large square of glass
that is this short-lease apartment's western window,
watching the older couple who live
on the same level in the neighbouring high-rise.

They always seem to be in view:
one of them sitting in a chair,
one of them plodding between rooms,
as if they're making an effort
to put on a show for me. Perhaps
they're thinking the same thing
when they look this way and see
I'm still here, seated at one end
of this foldout table, facing my screen.
I do my best to look busy. Yesterday

I watched them do the breakfast dishes:
the old man's forearm moving in circles
around and around as he scrubbed the plates,
the old lady waiting patiently beside him,
the tea towel draped over her arm.

Every afternoon they sit together on the sofa
in their conservatory, facing the empty beach,
filling in the crossword from the morning paper.
If tomorrow's forecast holds good,
and the winter sun returns,
perhaps they'll open their ranch slider
to the balcony and eat lunch al fresco.

Floral wallpaper

Doorways let light, people and weather
in and out, but it's the efforts of a pair
of silver candlesticks, along with
the statement of that occasional chair,
that truly make the room. That

and the twinned, gilt-surround mirrors,
set up in opposition, reflecting everything
to eternity. We made our decisions
about the décor, but in the end
any home boils down to one of two options:
the place you're on your way back to
or the place you're leaving.
All these years living in the yellow glare
of those entwined fake dahlias and now
here we are, stripping it back

over coffee, the French press diplomatically
tabled midway between us, doing our best
to leave the children out of this, those children
who anyway were never really ours,
who aren't even real children anymore.

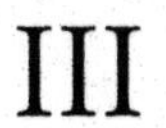

The great outdoors

Sitting on the step watching the trees
losing their extravagant ballgowns
to the breeze, I think how hard
it's going to be, getting used to all
the extra light again, like a parrot
in a cage with the cover left off.

Autumn is all about self-destruction.
Deciduous plants, detecting winter's approach,
send subtle signals down the lines: your services,
once highly valued, are no longer required.
For the leaves, it's hormonal, entirely natural,
this process of detachment from the host.
It's not external factors so much as the tree itself
bringing about the change. This morning

the smoke rises, sinuous, from between
my fingers, and a bright green grass snake
answers a call to move among the pots
on the patio, a leisurely glide. I shift
my corduroy legs aside to allow it
unhampered passage. Harmless, I know,

but there's still that shiver at the subtle slide.
And now there is some sort of gnat
humming, hovering unpleasantly close.
The famed French entomologist, Fabre,
who gave his life to the study of insects
said, at the end, that life is full of secrets,
that no one would ever learn
the last word concerning the gnat.

Follow the leader

Marginalia all over the place
and none of it making sense.
Lord knows I've tried, but

it's harder to be dynamic
than you'd think
from what it says on the packet

and for sure some of us will not
last the week. I like to pretend
no one knows I'm here,

that there's been a logistical
oversight. Long-term,
I'm hoping to be relieved

of command, allowed to stay
huddled behind this high wall
with my loaf of bread and my violin.

Herd

Interestingly, zebras don't suffer from stress
the stress researcher says. Immediately
I find myself worrying at her analysis.
Surely being pursued by a ravenous big cat
would be stressful? I imagine
under such circumstances even
the fastest in the herd would experience
some degree of anxiety? It turns out
relatively little research has been conducted into
those quiet moments after the danger has passed.
If only the survivors could tell us
how they're feeling. Recently captured footage
shows them glancing obliquely at one another
before hurriedly looking away again.

Seen

most days scattering crusts
for the pigeons; old man,
don't you know bread
is not what birds need to thrive?

Your face lately has been too grey
and too thin and, now I think of it,
I've not seen you for days.
Maybe you're lying

on your cold kitchen floor. Probably
you have a sign up: no junk mail,
please. But this afternoon
one of your neighbours will

surely notice your curtains still
drawn, will knock on your door.
Although, if your flat is at the far
end of a dead-end row, perhaps

no one passes from one week
to the next. That's maybe the thing
you like best about your flat. Maybe
that's what I'll like best about mine.

Burning with a low blue flame

In the thematic index of *The Dictionary of American Slang*,
the ways to say *drunk* take up nearly a page,

outnumbering those for *high* four to one. Taking out a half page
each, *stupid person* and *vomit* do better than most, whereas

there are barely a handful of listings for *annoying*, fewer still,
surprisingly, for *breasts* (*naughty bits* being

one of the tamer suggestions). *Excellent* garners half a column,
friend and *flee* manage a quarter page each,

fail (*tank, tube, flub the bub, go belly up*) a scant inch,
goodbye (*write if you get work*) almost two.

Good-looking from a distance has one entry (*Monet*).
Love has only *heart*; curiously, *lust* doesn't feature at all.

Denial

There's no show
without Punch. No rest
for the wicked, no time
like the present. No news
is good news.
No questions asked, no network access.
No spring chicken. No meat,
no dairy, no eggs. No more cakes and ale.
No such thing as a free lunch.
No left turn. No leg to stand on,
no country for old men, no quarter given.
Close,
but no cigar.
No smoke without fire,
no place like home. No sweat. No room
to swing a cat. No good deed
goes unpunished.
No hot water. No big deal. No means
no. No jail time. No laughing
matter. No running, no diving,
no bombs.
No strings attached, no pain
no gain. No turning back. Yes,
we have no bananas.
No dice.
No hard feelings. No time
to waste. No room
at the inn, no time
to explain.

No truck with that. Look Mum,
no hands. No man is an island.
No joke. No brainer. No ifs
or buts, no two ways about it.

Stronger this year

November winds are back, and you know
what that means, we mutter, not knowing
what we mean, it's just what we say

these days, while we're busy tracing
flattering images of ourselves onto walls
or carving enormous wooden effigies: great,

gormless dolls with incongruously delicate
hands and feet. Soon all will be concluded,
flamed like a slosh of brandy, whoosh, in a pan.

The moon's flat face hangs resigned,
just another cynic who knows we cannot hope
to score in the time remaining. Still, we persist

in singing the team songs our fathers taught us.
Yes! Keep going my son! we bellow, numb-punching
each other's arms. Don't dare stop, you hear?

Not until the covers are all dragged over,
not until every last old boy is tucked up
warm in the clubhouse.

Wednesday evening, around nine

Certain of our gold-leaf age, we remain
pretty unconvinced by the news
that tonight's sunset, seen through wide windows
framed by Laura Ashley chintz, will be our last.

We didn't foresee finding ourselves here,
sipping rum-based fruit cocktails, still
not really believing we're about to be taken out
by a rogue meteor predestined for millennia
to bury its ice-heavy head in this nondescript corner.

I guess this will be our very own archaeological moment,
you say (and I can tell you're impressed
by your own machismo), our great abridgement.
You, me, and Laura's lily o' the valley print.

All stations

We are on the ice
and are sinking
head down

Fool
You fool
Stand by

We are putting the real work off in the boats
We are putting practical solutions off in small boats

Stop talking
Keep out
Come quick

Emergency room flooded
Entire regions flooded

Global and climate security in boats
Cannot last much longer

Losing power
Sinking fast

This is *Titanic*
This is *Titanic*

Chipping away since 1893

Them women need to be less worried about the vote and more worried about their husband's dinner
Them women need to be less worried about the vote and more worried about their husbands
Them women need to be less worried about the vote and more worried about their
Them women need to be less worried about the vote and more worried about
Them women need to be less worried about the vote and more worried
Them women need to be less worried about the vote and more
Them women need to be less worried about the vote and
Them women need to be less worried about the vote
Them women need to be less worried about the
Them women need to be less worried about
Them women need to be less worried
Them women need to be less
Them women need to be
Them women need to
Them women need
Them women
Them

You could sell your lyrics

You could've been mine if you'd played your cards right.
You shouldn't have kissed me, that night. You might
like me better once you get to know me. You'll make
someone a great wife. You'd like that, wouldn't you?
You may not sing in the bathtub. You wouldn't hit a guy
with glasses. You might as well. You might be a tease
and not even know it. You shouldn't have done that,
he's just a boy. You could have seen this coming.
You should have woken me up. You should have
told me you were unhappy. You should have left me
when you had the chance. You couldn't make this shit up.
You could drive a person crazy, you know. You may not
find things as you left them. You may not like what you find.
You should have let me sleep. You should have let me
make it up to you. You might not fail on the scale I did.
You can make do with that. You can make that work.
You might get out of here alive. You can drive the getaway car.

A short lecture

From here (from there?)
it's harder to build, hence
more pots. Medium –
marble and bronze.
Bronze less lasting,
can be melted down
and reused. Correct
mistakes. Simple patterns
to fill up the space.
Sacred architecture –
as long as it is in use – will
keep being rebuilt. Very difficult,
telling the difference,
pinning it to a year,
a specific date. Black figure,
red figure; shoulder handled
male ash urn, belly handled
female; pyxis – a trinket box.
The wheel of life, as used
here, is purely decorative.

Beside the lake

The dog, as always, was keen to go on
but we could not see a path around
so stopped on the edge
and looked at the water,
the reflection of the trees
symmetrical and neat. Half your face,
the half turned towards me,
was in darkness. The other half,
on the other side of your nose,
was glowing in the lowering rays of the sun.
The dog sat at your feet, perhaps
even on your feet, leaning
into your legs, one fluffy ear cocked,
as if he could hear something
we couldn't moving between
the trees. You rested your hand
in the deep, soft fur at his neck.

Landscape

The backyard is a mess of cracked and crumbling
concrete kerbs left over from the people before us
and the ones before them, who apparently had big dreams
for this small space. Tonight there's just enough light
filtering through the frosted bathroom window
of the house over the fence to make long shadows
of the raised edges where once were flowerbeds,
the dark channel that was a storm drain, now half filled in.
When it rains, as it did all day today, everything washes
soft and liquid, and it feels as if all this could change
into someone else's backyard, someone with a fishpond
and a vege patch, a crazy paving patio edged
with deep blue hydrangeas. I've always hankered after
hydrangeas like my nana's, but they never grow well
for me, no matter what kind of shit I dig into the soil.

The condition of knowing

All my friends are dying –
poison dabbed onto the rims of cups,
heavy weights falling from
carefully contrived positions
above doorways,
the guard-rails designed to shield us from sheer cliffs
sawn through
then artfully balanced back in place.
Just now I was driving with Geoff, he was
sitting right next to me in the passenger seat,
when a bullet pierced the windshield.

Oh boy

Breaking a soft, yellow heart
with the edge of my fork, I recall
the shallow earthenware bowl
that always sat upon your windowsill,
the paint flaking off the window frame,
the dark beneath hinting at the beginning
of rot setting in and, beyond the glass,
the trees, blurry with condensation.
But they are outside and you are in the room
again, peering through your lens
at a single, faintly speckled specimen,
secure in its shell and placed precisely,
snug against the bowl's rim so it stays
still, serene, aglow with pale promise.

Notes

'Results sorted by relevance' is composed from selected titles held by Massey University's library.

'All stations' corrupts messages transmitted and received by the wireless operator aboard *Titanic* the night she sank.

'A short lecture' owes its existence to notes taken by Finn O'Neill-Stevens.

Acknowledgements

Thank you to the editors of the following publications where versions of some of these poems first appeared: *The Interpreter's House*, *Landfall*, *Mayhem*, *Overground Underground*, *Poetry Aotearoa Yearbook*, *Sport*, *Turbine / Kapohau*. Many thanks to Jon Stone and Kirsten Irving of Sidekick Books for including my work in their wonderful *Hipflask* series. Appreciation to the Hawthornden Literary Retreat for the gift of the month-long fellowship, where a number of these poems were created.

Thank you to Morgan Bach and Helena Wiśniewska Brow for camaraderie and help with the poems. Thanks to James Brown for taking tea and talking poetry. Thank you to Ruby, Ashleigh, Fergus and all the team at Te Herenga Waka University Press for their support in bringing this book into being. Gratitude to Catherine, Hana, Tanya, Kathryn, Viv and Gavin for enduring friendship and good times. Thank you to the members of my family who provide support (and occasional inspiration), especially Mum, who's been my number one fan my whole life. Above all, I'm forever grateful to Greg for always cheering me on in my dreams and schemes.